BATTLING DINOSAURS

How to use the app

Discover an amazing world with Augmented Reality

This book, together with the free app, uses the very latest Augmented Reality (AR) technology to mix the real and virtual worlds together. Viewed through your mobile device, the battling dinosaurs will appear to come to life as interactive animations.

Wow! What do I need?

To run the Augmented Reality animations, all you need is this book, the app and a mobile device that meets the minimum requirement specification below.

This product will work with the following devices:

• The following Apple devices running iOS 6.0 or above: iPhone 4S or above; iPad2 or above; iPod Touch 5th Gen. or above.

• Android devices with both forward- and backward-facing cameras using Android 4.0 and above, and ARMv7 processors - INTEL based devices are not supported.

• Battle mode will require an active wi-fi connection.

It's easy! Here's what you need to do...

1 Download the free iBattleAR app from www.apple.com/itunes or www.android.com.apps to your mobile device. Open the app and go to the home page.

2 Tap the iBattleAR button to activate the AR and discover 5 FREE fierce dinosaurs. There are 2 modes to choose from: Single User 👤 and Battle Mode ⚔.

3 Each of the 13 dinosaurs in the book has their own Activation Page. Select a mode, then hold your mobile device over one of the Activation Pages to release incredible Augmented Reality dinosaurs!

4 Take photographs of your dinosaurs with your friends, as they explore your home or while fighting other dinosaurs. The Camera button 📷 lets you save to your photo album to share later.

Watch your dinosaur run across your room and check out each dinosaur's special features.

Step 1 – Select the Single User mode, tap the **Start button** and your camera will automatically activate. View any of the Activation Pages to make the dinosaur appear.

Step 2 – Use the onscreen **joystick** to make your dinosaur walk around and hear it roar. Take a picture of your dinosaur with the **Camera button**.

Once you get used to the controls, try walking your dinosaur off the page and further away. Try out different angles or hold your device up close to see amazing detail.

NEED SOME HELP?
Check out our useful website for helpful tips and problem-solving advice:

www.carltonbooks.co.uk/icarltonbooks/help

Grab a friend with a second device to battle your dinosaurs. Each contestant needs to trigger a dinosaur using the free app and AR, then let the battle begin!

Step 1 – Both users open the app on their device and select Battle Mode.

Step 2 – The first user taps the **Start button** and selects their dinosaur from the on-screen menu. They then need to tap the **Play button** ▶ twice, and view THESE pages (How to use the app) to activate their AR dinosaur in the battle arena.

Step 3 – The second user taps the **Start button**, selects their dinosaur and taps the **Play button** ▶. They then select the first users device from the list of friends shown and views THESE pages to start the battle.

Step 4 – Each dinosaur has two moves. They can either **attack** ★ or **defend** ⬟. The dinosaurs will need to be near each other for these actions to work. You can move the dinosaurs by using the **joystick**.

Both users will see TWO dinosaurs on screen, but will only be able to control the dinosaur they selected. There is an energy ring underneath each dinosaur, which shows how much energy that dinosaur has. Once all the energy has been used up that dinosaur loses the battle.

The winner is the dinosaur that survives!

USING iBattleAR APP

Five Free Dinosaurs:
Tyrannosaurus Rex
Cryolophosaurus
Velociraptor
Herrerasaurus
Deinonychus

If you want to unlock more dinosaurs you can purchase your favourites using the In-App Purchase Facility available on the main menu under the shopping trolley icon 🛒. There are two different dinosaur packs to purchase, each contains four ferocious dinosaurs. Or you can purchase the Monster Pack that includes all eight extra dinosaurs for a special price!

Four More Dinosaurs with Pack 1:
Utahraptor
Spinosaurus
Megalosaurus
Albertosaurus

Four More Dinosaurs with Pack 2:
Giganotosaurus
Allosaurus
Maposaurus
Carcharodontosaurus

UTAHRAPTOR

This carnivorous creature didn't have to rely on its jaws and teeth to attack – it had two huge dangerous hooked claws on its feet to slash at prey. Combined with a quick top speed, this dinosaur was a terrifying predator.

FEATHERS NOT FUR

Being covered in feathers provided Utahraptor with camouflage in the woodlands where it hunted. It had a fan of feathers growing out of its bony tail to help it balance – very useful for when it was standing on one foot and using the other to kick or stab its prey.

STAB AND SLICE

Utahraptor's sickle-shaped claws on the second toe of each foot were up to 25 centimetres long. These deadly weapons were used like a knife to stab at prey, and the hooked shape meant they could slice flesh off a carcass with one swift move.

SPEED OVER SIZE

At only 7 metres long, this dinosaur wasn't going to outdo the likes of T. rex or Giganotosaurus for sheer presence. But its short, muscular legs gave it power and speed – a deadly combo when pursuing prey.

SERRATED TEETH

A powerful jaw filled with teeth is only good if you know how to use it! Utahraptor's teeth were serrated, meaning they could saw through thick chunks of meat it had sliced off prey with its claws.

DINO BATTLE

☆ CONTENDER No.1 ☆

NAME	UTAHRAPTOR
	(You-tah-RAP-tor)
LENGTH	7 metres / 23 feet
WEIGHT	700 kilograms / 1,543 pounds
SPEED	48 km/h / 30 mph

KEY ATTACKING MOVES

• Speed • Claw stab

BATTLE STATS

ATTACK	Claws, jaws	7/10
DEFENCE	Speed, camouflage	8/10
X-FACTOR	Two huge claws on feet	8/10

PREDATOR BATTLE RATING 88%

TYRANNOSAURUS REX

Does the king of the dinosaurs deserve such a title? Huge jaws, pointed teeth, thick tail, powerful muscles and sharp claws – lots of predators share these features. What makes T. rex the undisputed king was its ferocious killer attitude.

CLEVER CLOGS

T. rex was smart. It knew what it was doing and its ruthless attitude was combined with acute hearing and keen eyesight. No other dinosaur could outsmart T. rex and this is why it remains one of the most deadly predators ever.

SENSE OF SMELL

Scientists have recently revealed that T. rex had a superior sense of smell. This meant it was likely to hunt at night as well as during the day, and it could navigate through large areas by sniffing out its next victim. It seems there really was nowhere to hide for the prey of this fearsome beast.

POWER GRIP

Although its arms were short, size doesn't always matter. The power grip and sharp claws these arms provided meant they were a secret weapon, used for holding down prey or slashing through skin.

HEADS ABOVE

Tyrannosaurus rex's head was its most striking feature. It had huge shoulder muscles to support the weight of its heavy head. While its teeth were on show, the real power was hidden away – the roof of its mouth was made of thick, hard bone and helped to create that mega bite.

DINO BATTLE
★ CONTENDER No.2 ★

NAME	TYRANNOSAURUS REX *(Tie-ran-oh-SAW-us rex)*
LENGTH	12 metres / 39.4 feet
WEIGHT	6 tonnes / 6.6 tons
SPEED	29 km/h / 18 mph

KEY ATTACKING MOVES

- Bite
- Body slam

BATTLE STATS

ATTACK Jaws, teeth, high IQ **9/10**

DEFENCE Superior sense of smell, size **7/10**

X-FACTOR Ferocious killer **9/10**

PREDATOR BATTLE RATING **92%**

SPINOSAURUS

This huge predator is up for the award of biggest and best. With the speed of a T. rex, the jaws of a crocodile and the body length of two buses, Spinosaurus had a killer combination of weapons.

SUPER SAIL

You wouldn't miss this dinosaur heading towards you with the super-sized sail on its back. Scientists think the sail was used to help control body temperature, as blood could flow close to the surface of the skin here to warm up or cool down. It also made this dinosaur very intimidating!

LEGS AND CLAWS

Like other theropods, Spinosaurus walked on its two back legs. These powerful limbs meant it could run at speeds of up to 32 km/h. Its forearms were also long enough to enable it to walk on all fours, unlike T. rex. At the end of each limb were three sharp claws, hooked so they could tear off chunks of meat.

TEETH AND JAWS

Spinosaurus' jaws were its primary weapon. Its head could grow up to 1.8 metres long, meaning it could easily grab prey with one bite. The jaw was lined with long, sharp teeth, perfect for holding on to slippery fish as it moved through the swamps.

LAND AND WATER

Spinosaurus lived in North Africa, on land that is now Egypt and Morocco. Its status as a top predator comes from the fact that it felt at home in the water as well as on land. It would often be found wading through swamps and lagoons, so there was no easy escape for prey.

DINO BATTLE
☆ CONTENDER No.3 ☆

NAME	SPINOSAURUS *(Spine-oh-SORE-us)*
LENGTH	18 metres / 59.1 feet
WEIGHT	10 tonnes / 11 tons
SPEED	32 km/h / 20 mph

KEY ATTACKING MOVES
- Bite • Claw swipe

BATTLE STATS

ATTACK	Claws, jaws	9/10
DEFENCE	Size, able to swim	10/10
X-FACTOR	Huge sail on back	9/10

PREDATOR BATTLE RATING 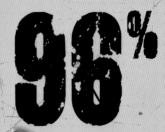 96%

VELOCIRAPTOR

Velociraptor was fearless – a good thing when you're a tiny predator playing with the big boys. Its speed, aggression and sharp, hooked claws more than made up for its lack of size.

RAPID ATTACK

With a top speed of 40 km/h, Velociraptor could approach prey swiftly and suddenly before its victim had even spotted any danger. Small and agile, this dinosaur was found darting around the open plains of eastern Asia.

DEADLY DAGGERS

The two sickle-shaped claws on the third toe of each foot were like daggers. Velociraptor would lift them off the ground when running and then, in one quick movement, leap onto its prey and insert the daggers, creating a terrible wound.

NIGHT VISION

Velociraptor's eyes were adapted for hunting in low light. Fossils show that it had the same eye shape and size as modern animals that prowl at night. This meant it could hunt when it had the cover of darkness to protect it from larger beasts.

BIRD-LIKE LOOKS

Velociraptor had a long, low, flat skull and an upturned snout. Its 60 teeth were small and sharp, perfect for tearing flesh. Its body was covered in short feathers with longer ones on the arms and tail. But you can be sure it was a dinosaur not a bird!

DINO BATTLE
★ CONTENDER No.4 ★

NAME	VELOCIRAPTOR *(Veh-loss-ee-RAP-tor)*
LENGTH	2 metres / 6.6 feet
WEIGHT	15 kilograms / 33 pounds
SPEED	40 km/h / 25 mph

KEY ATTACKING MOVES
- Speed • Claw stab

BATTLE STATS

ATTACK	Claws, sharp teeth	**6/10**
DEFENCE	Speed, good eyesight	**7/10**
X-FACTOR	High IQ, group attack	**8/10**

PREDATOR BATTLE RATING **80%**

MEGALOSAURUS

Its name means 'giant lizard' and it was the first dinosaur to be recognized by scientists. This predator is known for its powerful arms and strong grip, key features for a deadly killer.

BRITISH BEAST

Megalosaurus lived in the forests of what is now Britain during the Mid Jurassic Period. Trees and undergrowth meant it would stalk its prey carefully before reaching out to grab, hold and then deliver the bite.

BIG HEAD

A massive head and long jaws show Megalosaurus was a classic carnivore. It had dagger-like teeth ready to slice through flesh. A solid lower jaw suggests it had a bite to rival T. rex.

POWER GRIP

Megalosaurus would have been good at tug of war — once it grabbed onto something it didn't let go! Strong arms, longer than dinosaurs of a similar build, had three long claws at the end so it could grab and pin prey.

DINO BATTLE
☆ **CONTENDER No.5** ☆

NAME	MEGALOSAURUS
	(Meg-ah-lo-SAW-rus)
LENGTH	6 metres / 19.7 feet
WEIGHT	700 kilograms / 1,543 pounds
SPEED	48 km/h / 30 mph

KEY ATTACKING MOVES
- Bite • Strong grip

BATTLE STATS

ATTACK	Jaws, strength	6/10
DEFENCE	Speed	5/10
X-FACTOR	Powerful grip	7/10

PREDATOR BATTLE RATING 76%

TWO OR FOUR?
When it was first discovered, scientists thought this dinosaur walked on four legs, like modern lizards. But like other predatory theropods ('beast-footed' dinosaurs), Megalosaurus actually walked on two legs, had a horizontal torso and used its tail for balance.

HERRERASAURUS

Herrerasaurus was the number one dinosaur in South America during the Triassic Period. At 4 metres long it was the biggest beast in its class and it had the pick of the region's smaller dinosaurs.

MUSCLE WORKOUT
Big muscles don't come naturally, and early reptiles didn't all have strong, powerful bodies. Herrerasaurus marked the start of the rise of the mega beasts – those with big muscles were better hunters and lived longer, so they were natural survivors.

DAYLIGHT SPRINTER
Scientists believe that Herrerasaurus was active during the day for short periods of time. With a top speed of 48 km/h this probably means it was a sprint champion.

RIVALS

Even the very top predators have rivals. Herrerasaurus' rival was Saurosuchus — a giant crocodile-like reptile that was around 7 metres long and walked on all four legs.

DINO BATTLE

☆ CONTENDER No.6 ☆

NAME	HERRERASAURUS
	(Er-air-uh-SAW-rus)
LENGTH	4 metres / 13.1 feet
WEIGHT	200 kilograms / 441 pounds
SPEED	48 km/h / 30 mph

KEY ATTACKING MOVES

• Claw swipe • Teeth slice

BATTLE STATS

ATTACK	Strength, claws, teeth	**6/10**
DEFENCE	Speed	**5/10**
X-FACTOR	Strong muscles	**6/10**

PREDATOR BATTLE RATING  **75%**

CURVED TEETH

Herrerasaurus had 80 curved, serrated teeth. The serrations meant it could rip up flesh, and the curved teeth meant that if it grabbed prey whole, it wouldn't slide out of its mouth by mistake when running.

GIGANOTOSAURUS

The clue is in the name with this dinosaur. Giant Giganotosaurus was 12.5 metres long and weighed 8 tonnes. It looked like a larger version of T. rex, but luckily Giganotosaurus lived in South America and T. rex in North America.

BONY HEAD

Bony lumps and ridges on the top of the head protected the skull and eyes from bumps. This would have made the head very heavy, and at the size of a human, it's a good job Giganotosaurus had a strong neck to support it.

BULLDOZER

With a body the size of Giganotosaurus, you don't really need weapons! This beast could simply body slam its prey, pushing it to the ground and knocking it senseless.

ANY ARMS?

Under that huge body it was hard to see Giganotosaurus' tiny arms! They were short and weak, but long sharp claws at the end of all six fingers meant it could swipe at prey when needed.

AIM BIG

Giganotosaurus liked to surprise its prey by bursting out of the tall South American trees. Sometimes it would even take on the biggest of the giant plant-eating sauropods by teaming up with a family member.

DINO BATTLE
★ CONTENDER No.7 ★

NAME	GIGANOTOSAURUS
	(Jig-ah-no-toh-SAW-rus)
LENGTH	12.5 metres / 41 feet
WEIGHT	8 tonnes / 8.8 tons
SPEED	30 km/h / 19 mph

KEY ATTACKING MOVES
- Bite • Body slam

BATTLE STATS

ATTACK	Teeth, jaws, body slam
	surprise attack **10/10**
DEFENCE	Size **8/10**
X-FACTOR	Enormous size **8/10**

PREDATOR BATTLE RATING 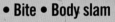 93%

DEINONYCHUS

This predator is all about speed. Small and light, it lived in what is now the USA during the Early Cretaceous Period. This creature looked a bit like a bird, with the deadly jaws of a meat-eating dinosaur.

RUN AND JUMP

The advantage of being small was that Deinonychus could leap into the air – you wouldn't see Giganotosaurus doing that! This predator would run towards prey bigger than itself and jump onto its back. The claws would then inflict wounds and Deinonychus' bite would finish the battle.

TOP SPEED

With a top speed of 56 km/h, Deinonychus was a sprinter. It had strong leg muscles and a streamlined shape to allow it to run and attack prey like a bullet. Its long tail helped it balance when turning at speed.

SMALL, SHARP TEETH

Due to its size, Deinonychus did not have a strong bite. Instead it had a mouth filled with lots of small, sharp teeth. Slotted close together they could pierce flesh upon contact and cause a fatal wound for the prey.

TERRIBLE CLAW

Deinonychus means 'terrible claw', and this creature lives up to its name with a huge, curved claw on the middle toe of each foot. The claw was used to pierce the skin of prey and then rip the flesh apart. Truly terrible!

DINO BATTLE
☆ CONTENDER No.8 ☆

NAME	DEINONYCHUS
	(Dine-oh-NYE-chus)
LENGTH	3 metres / 9.8 feet
WEIGHT	60 kilograms / 132 pounds
SPEED	56 km/h / 35 mph

KEY ATTACKING MOVES
• Speed • Jump

BATTLE STATS

ATTACK	Teeth, claws, jump 7/10
DEFENCE	Speed 8/10
X-FACTOR	Lightning-fast speed 9/10

PREDATOR BATTLE RATING 90%

CRYOLOPHOSAURUS

The predatory theropods of the Jurassic Period often looked the same. Cryolophosaurus stood out from the crowd, though, as it had a special feature that would turn heads. Imagine coming face-to-face with those jaws, head crest and horns!

COOL CARNIVORE

This dinosaur was one cool creature – its fossils were found just 650 kilometres from what is now the South Pole. It is the most southerly dinosaur ever discovered. But it wouldn't have been stomping about in the snow, as temperatures were warmer in the Early Jurassic Period than they are today.

TAIL WHIP

Cryolophosaurus had a long, thick tail that could knock out smaller prey with one flick. Almost as long as the dinosaur's body, it would also have helped balance the heavy head.

STRONG JAWS

Strong jaws filled with teeth would have been used to kill prey, but also to devour animals that were already dead. Just because Cryolophosaurus had a killer instinct, that doesn't mean it would have passed up a ready-prepared meal!

ELVISAURUS

Cryolophosaurus had a stylish head crest that looked like a pop star's quiff! It had distinctive grooves, was shaped like a fan and was probably brightly coloured so it could be used to attract a mate, or create a scary territorial display to ward off rivals.

DINO BATTLE
★ CONTENDER No.9 ★

NAME	CRYOLOPHOSAURUS
	(Cry-oh-loaf-oh-SAW-rus)
LENGTH	6 metres / 19.7 feet
WEIGHT	450 kilograms / 992 pounds
SPEED	24 km/h / 15 mph

KEY ATTACKING MOVES
- Bite • Tail swing

BATTLE STATS

ATTACK	Claws, teeth, strength	**6/10**
DEFENCE	Tail, head crest	**7/10**
X-FACTOR	Fan-shaped head crest	**7/10**

PREDATOR BATTLE RATING 78%

MAPUSAURUS

Fossils of Mapusaurus were excavated between 1997 and 2001 in Argentina. Scientists discovered a bone bed containing at least seven individuals which suggests this mean predator hunted in packs.

GROUP WORK

Before discovering Mapusaurus, it was thought that meat-eating dinosaurs hunted alone. The fact that Mapusaurus hunted in groups meant it had no limit on its choice of prey. Three of these clever beasts could easily bring down a huge plant-eater – a real feast for the family!

TEETH LIKE KNIVES

Mapusaurus' teeth were designed for slicing through flesh rather than crushing bones. Its jaw was more delicate than T. rex's, suggesting that it preferred to wound prey and wait for it to die rather than killing it with a single bite.

LONG CLAWS

Mapusaurus had long, strong back legs but short arms. All fingers and toes had a claw – the ones on the feet would have been used for kicking and stabbing and the ones on the hands used for grabbing and slicing.

DINO BATTLE
★ CONTENDER No.10 ★

NAME MAPUSAURUS
(MAP-puh-saw-rus)
LENGTH 12 metres / 39.4 feet
WEIGHT 6 tonnes / 6.6 tons
SPEED 25 km/h / 15.5 mph

KEY ATTACKING MOVES
• Group attack • Claw swipe

BATTLE STATS

ATTACK Teeth, claw swipe **6/10**
DEFENCE Size **8/10**
X-FACTOR Attacked as a group **8/10**

PREDATOR BATTLE RATING **85%**

BIG AND BULKY
Mapusaurus was big, close to Giganotosaurus in size, at 12 metres long. Being built like a bus meant it didn't have a high top speed, but it was solid and could easily shrug off any attacks against it.

ALLOSAURUS

This dinosaur was a common killer during the Late Jurassic Period. It was clever and built to attack prey smaller than itself – at 10 metres long that meant it had a lot of choice!

FOOD, GLORIOUS FOOD

Allosaurus loved to eat meat and would stop at nothing to get a meal. It was a scavenger as well as a hunter. Favourite dishes included Camptosaurus, Stegosaurus and young sauropods.

AMBUSH ATTACK

Being so big meant Allosaurus couldn't run at top speed for long. Its favourite method of attack was to ambush prey, taking it by surprise. This way it only required one quick tail swipe or body slam to knock prey down, before going in for the kill.

AXE-LIKE SKULL

Allosaurus had a relatively weak bite, but its jaws were double hinged meaning it could open its mouth really wide. Its skull could withstand huge forces and it used its head like an axe.

NEW TEETH

Crunching through bones and eating huge chunks of meat meant even the strongest of Allosaurus' curved teeth would wear down over time. But it grew new teeth throughout its life and if a tooth was knocked out in a fight, a new one would soon grow to fill the gap.

DINO BATTLE
★ CONTENDER No.11 ★

NAME	ALLOSAURUS (Al-owe-SAW-rus)
LENGTH	10 metres / 32.8 feet
WEIGHT	2.5 tonnes / 2.76 tons
SPEED	35 km/h / 22 mph

KEY ATTACKING MOVES
- Claw stab • Tail swing

BATTLE STATS

ATTACK	Claws, jaws	7/10
DEFENCE	Size, large hands	7/10
X-FACTOR	Backwards-curving teeth to hold prey	5/10

PREDATOR BATTLE RATING 81%

CARCHARODONTOSAURUS

This enormous killer was one to watch. Weighing in at 7 tonnes and measuring 13 metres, it was huge. Its teeth were its main weapon – at 16 centimetres long, serrated and curved, there was nothing they couldn't cut through.

GREAT WHITE

Carcharodontosaurus' teeth look much like a great white shark's, and we all know what damage they can do! In fact, the first half of this dinosaur's name – 'Carcharodon' – is the same as the great white shark's scientific name.

GOOD EYESIGHT

Dinosaurs had small brains and slow senses compared with human standards. But it is believed Carcharodontosaurus had good stereoscopic vision, meaning it could use depth perception to work out the distance between itself and its prey.

TERRITORIAL

A big dinosaur needs a big hunting range, but competition for the best patch of land was fierce. Rival males would fight to secure their territory and bite marks on the fossils of jawbones show they were prepared to fight to the death.

BATTLE TO BE THE BEST

Scientists think that Carcharodontosaurus would have done battle with Spinosaurus. The two largest carnivores went head-to-head in the Mid Cretaceous Period. This was a battle of size and power against bite and it was often too close to predict the outcome.

DINO BATTLE
★ CONTENDER No.12 ★

NAME	CARCHARODONTOSAURUS
	(Kahr-KAR-o-DON-to-SAW-rus)
LENGTH	13 metres / 42.7 feet
WEIGHT	7 tonnes / 7.7 tons
SPEED	30 km/h / 19 mph

KEY ATTACKING MOVES
• Bite • Teeth slice

BATTLE STATS

ATTACK	Teeth, jaws	9/10
DEFENCE	Good eyesight, size	9/10
X-FACTOR	16 cm-long, serrated teeth	9/10

PREDATOR BATTLE RATING  95%

ALBERTOSAURUS

Albertosaurus was a top predator in western North America during the Late Cretaceous Period. It was smaller than its cousin, T. rex, but more aerodynamic and flexible.

SLOW AND STEADY

Albertosaurus wasn't exactly slow, but it wasn't known for being fast. Instead, it was able to run for longer than most of the large carnivores, a great advantage when competing for prey.

SEPTIC BITE

Like many dinosaurs, Albertosaurus had serrated teeth. Its teeth curved backwards though, meaning small pieces of meat may have stuck in the grooves and become home to deadly bacteria, giving it a septic bite.